Mediterranean
Wild~~~~s

ps

Martyn Rix
and Nicky Foy

Elm Tree Books London

INTRODUCTION

Aim

The aim of this book has been to photograph the most important and common plants of the Mediterranean region in order that the increasing number of visitors to the area will be able to distinguish and identify the flowers that they are most likely to come across in their travels. The whole Mediterranean region is covered from Spain, Morocco and North Africa in the west, to Turkey and the Middle East.

How to use this book

The book is arranged by season beginning with the earliest plants of spring and continuing through to the summer flowers and autumn bulbs. For most of the plants there are two photographs: one showing it in its natural habitat and the other showing it laid out in the manner of a botanical drawing so that the details can be observed. In many instances the plants found are rare and should not be picked, so in these cases the second photograph is usually a field close-up to show details.

The Mediterranean climate and habitat

What distinguishing characteristics of the Mediterranean region contribute to the richness and variety of plant life to be found there?

One outstanding feature is the climate. Plenty of rain-fall during all but the hot, dry, summer months and virtually no frost mean that numerous plants unable to endure a temperate climate can flourish.

Helichrysum stoechas near Narbonne

A second outstanding feature of the region is the dominance of the scrub habitat – the maquis. This terrain is characterised by a dense layer of evergreen shrubs which can sustain life in arid, rocky soil during hot, dry summers. It is in the clearings and on the edges of the maquis that many fascinating wild flowers of this region can be found.

The photographs

The studio photographs were taken on a Bronica 120 format with a 75 mm lens. Scale: ○ is 1 cm. The field photographs were taken on a Nikon FM camera with a 50 mm lens, occasionally with close-up attachments. The film was Kodak Ektachrome 64 ASA in both cases, but when used outdoors it was pushed one stop in development.

Glossary

anther	part of flower holding pollen
bract	a modified leaf beneath a flower head, or at the base of the flower stem
corm	bulb-like subterraneous stem
corolla	inner, usually green, parts of the flower
obovate	ovate but broader above the middle
procumbent	having a prostrate or trailing stem
spadix	a form of inflorescence consisting of a thick, fleshy spike, closely set with flowers, and enclosed in a spathe
spathe	a large bract or sheathing-leaf enveloping the inflorescence

Mimosa March 10

Silver Wattle or Mimosa

Acacia dealbata is an evergreen tree that grows best on sandy soil in warm places in gardens, roadsides and waste places. Found in southern Britain and throughout the Mediterranean, it is sometimes quite abundant particularly on the French Riviera. It can grow to 30 metres in the wild but more commonly it reaches 8–12 metres in cultivation. It flowers February to April.

Of Australian origin, the Silver Wattle has a smooth, white trunk and long leafy branches and is characterised by the silvery down that covers its compound, paired leaves and young shoots. The yellow flowers with their beautiful, fragrant scent grow in numerous, multi-branched clusters at the end of the branches. As it regenerates naturally and quickly by suckers this most beautiful wattle is often planted to stabilise the soil as well as for timber and ornament. Large quantities of the flowering branches are sold in shops as 'mimosa'.

Mimosa

Yellow Star-of-Bethlehem

Gagea chrysantha, (syn. *G. amblyopetala*), grows in mountain scrub and open woods and is found in the eastern Mediterranean region from Sicily and Yugoslavia and North Africa to Turkey. Up to 15 cm high, it flowers February to April.

This pretty bulb of the lily family has two narrow basal leaves, a smooth stem and shining yellow flowers. The buds hang down.

There are about twelve species of *Gagea* found around the Mediterranean region, differing from one another in the way their flowering stems branch and also in the number, thickness and hairiness of their basal leaves.

Gagea peduncularis is found in the eastern Mediterranean region from Bulgaria to Greece and Turkey. It can be recognised by the flat, narrow, basal leaves and the woolly stems and buds. Also it has bulbils at the base of the flowering stem.

Gagea peduncularis

Horseshoe Orchid, Greece April 1

Early Spider Orchid

Ophrys sphegodes grows on chalky soil in grasslands, woodland clearings and scrub. Widely distributed in France, Italy, Corsica, northern Greece and the Crimea, it is rare in southern Britain. 10–65 cm high, it flowers April to June or earlier in the south. A very variable species which has 3–10 flowers, it has an ovoid lip with a small hump on each side: maroon-brown with a bluish X- or H-shaped mark. The green, pointed sepals are rather long and narrow.

Horseshoe Orchid, *Ophrys ferrum-equinum*, grows on chalky soil in grassland among maquis and in pine forests. It is found in Greece, Crete, the Aegean Islands, Rhodes and Turkey. 15–30 cm high, it flowers March to May. The purplish-brown lip generally has a blue inverted horse-shoe marking. The pink sepals have green veins and the smaller, pink petals sometimes have wavy edges.

Early Spider Orchid, France April 19

Early Spider Orchid, Greece, April 3

Sawfly Orchid, Greece April 6

Sawfly Orchid

Ophrys tenthredinifera grows in grassy or stony areas in scrub or maquis and is widely distributed, but localised in Portugal, Spain, Italy, Greece, western Turkey and north Africa. 10–40 cm high, it flowers February to May. Note the large yellow, hairy lip with a red-brown area in the middle and small, blue, white-margined pattern near the base.

Woodcock Orchid, *Ophrys scolopax*, grows in chalky soil on scrubby hillsides and woodlands and is widely distributed throughout the Mediterranean region to central Greece. 8–45 cm high, it flowers March to May. A very variable species, but the rounded, reddish-brown lip with a pattern of lines and circles has a small, pointed tip at the apex; also the sepals and petals are pinky-red.

Ophrys scolopax ssp. *cornuta* is similar in colouring but has prolonged, forward-pointing side lobes on the lip. It is found from Yugoslavia to northern Turkey and flowers April to May.

Woodcock Orchid, France April 20

Ophrys scolopax ssp. *Cormita*, Greece

Bumble Bee Orchid, Greece April 5

Mirror Orchid or Mirror of Venus
Ophrys speculum grows in rocky, grassy areas, woodlands and maquis. It is widely distributed and sometimes locally common throughout the Mediterranean region. 10–30 cm high, it flowers March to April. The three-lobed lip has arm-like side lobes, a large, shining blue centre with a yellow border and is entirely edged with a red-brown to purplish hairy fringe. The narrow, green sepals have maroon stripes and the small, round petals are also maroon.

Bumble Bee Orchid, *Ophrys bombyliflora*, grows in short grassland and maquis and is widely distributed, though not common, throughout the Mediterranean region. 7–25 cm high, it flowers March to April. The broad, squarish purple-brown lip has prominent, hairy, lumpy side lobes and some shiny pale blue markings in the centre. Both sepals and petals are rounded and green. Note the new tubers are produced at the end of a long root.

12

Mirror Orchid, Greece March 30

Sombre Bee Orchid, Nice, France May 4

Yellow Bee Orchid

Ophrys lutea grows in grassy areas and maquis and is very commonly found throughout the Mediterranean region. 10–30 cm high, it flowers March to April and is easily recognised by its distinctive lip with well-developed side lobes and an indent at the top of the middle lobe. A broad yellow margin surrounds the central, red-brown area which is sometimes marked with bluish patches. *Ophrys lutea* var. *minor* is also common in the area but has a small central lobe and an inverted V at the base of the lip.

Sombre Bee Orchid, *Ophrys fusca*, grows in olive orchards, maquis, scrub and chalky or stony hillsides. One of the commonest and most widespread *Ophrys*, it is found throughout the Mediterranean region. 10–40 cm high, it flowers February to May. Again, easily recognised by its three-lobed lip, indented at the top of the central lobe, which is dark, almost black, edged with a narrow yellow or greenish margin and with two, blue, oval patches near the base.

Yellow Bee Orchid, Ronda, Spain May 1

Giant Orchid, Greece March 4

Giant Orchid

Barlia robertiana (synonym *Himantoglossum longibracteatum*) grows in thickets, grassy banks, woodland, scrubby hillsides and dry, stony places. It is widely distributed, and sometimes locally common throughout the Mediterranean region, extending to the Canary Islands. 30–70 cm high, it is one of the earliest orchids to flower, sometimes in late December, more usually about February to April.

This huge, thick-stemmed, broad-leaved orchid is extremely robust. The cylindrical flower spike is densely covered with numerous flowers. The three-lobed lip has sickle-shaped side lobes and a central lobe that divides into two short points – all parts have wavy edges and vary in colour from white-grey to green to red to purple with faint markings. The flowers usually, although not always, smell of lily-of-the-valley. The side sepals spread like 'ears', the back sepal and petals curve inwards to form a sort of loose helmet.

Giant Orchid, France March 21

Loose-flowered Orchid, Greece April 3

Loose-flowered Orchid

Orchis laxiflora grows in marshy meadows, ditches, bogs and damp, sandy places. It is widely distributed throughout the Mediterranean region and as far north as the Channel Islands. 30–50 cm and occasionally 100 cm high, it flowers April to June.

7–10 spear-shaped, channelled leaves point upwards to a long, loose spike of between 6 and 20 flowers. The rounded lip is slightly three-lobed with the side lobes much larger than the central one. The flowers are generally strong red to mauve-red and more occasionally pink or, rarely, white. The sepals are outward spreading while the petals curve inwards to form a loose hood.

Orchis laxiflora ssp. *palustris* is very similar but the lip is distinctly three-lobed with the central lobe being as long or longer than the side lobes. It is more magenta-coloured with a white centre and small purplish markings.

Loose-flowered Orchid, Greece April 3

Giant Fennel, Turkey April 30

Giant Fennel

Ferula communis, a robust, herbaceous perennial, is commonly found in limestone on dry hillsides. 2–5 metres high, it flowers March to June.

The very thick, hollow stem is often branched and the soft, bright green, feathery leaves are divided many times into thread-like lobes. The leaves die down in summer to reappear in the autumn. The flowering stem has many large yellow umbels and the elliptical shaped fruit is flattened with thin, side rings.

Smyrnium rotundifolium, a biennial, grows in olive orchards and bushy places and is found from Italy east to Turkey. 30–60 cm high, it flowers April to June. This bright green, leafy plant has orb-shaped upper leaves with smooth margins (or rarely, very slightly toothed) and stems. The yellow-flowered umbels have 7 to 12 rays and the tiny fruit is black when ripe.

Biennial Alexanders, *Smyrnium perfoliatum*, is very similar but has furrowed stems and oval-shaped leaves with a toothed margin.

Biennial Alexanders photographed April 23

Pink Butterfly Orchid, Ronda, Spain April 30

Pink Butterfly Orchid

Orchis papilionacea grows in dry, sunny places like open woodland and maquis among shrubs and grass, preferring calcareous or slightly acid soil. It is quite common and found widely distributed throughout the Mediterranean region and northwards to the Caucasus. 10–35 cm high, it flowers March to May.

This wonderful orchid has long, spear-shaped, grooved leaves on an angular stem and a loose cluster of 3 to 10 flowers. The sepals and petals form a large, loose hood and the large, unlobed lip is fan-shaped with a toothed edge. It is generally paler than the hood and streaked with darker red lines. As seen here the colours can vary from deep mauve-red to pink to white.

Orchis papilionacea ssp. *bruhnsiana* has a smaller, spoon-shaped lip and is found only in Transcaucasia.

Pink Butterfly Orchid (white form), Greece April 8

Pink Butterfly Orchid, Greece April 9

Naked Man Orchid (white form), Greece April 10

Naked Man Orchid

Orchis italica grows in open woodlands, pine woods, maquis and grassy or stony areas, preferring calcareous soils. A common species, it is widely distributed in the Mediterranean region. 20–50 cm high, it flowers March to May.

This tall, striking orchid has long, spear-shaped leaves with wavy edges which are sometimes spotted. It has a fairly dense flower cluster which flowers from the bottom upwards and each looks like a little man – the sepals and petals forming a head-like hood; the narrow, downward-pointing side lobes representing arms and the deeply split central lobe with a narrow pointed tooth in the middle represents legs and penis. Generally the pinky red hood is streaked with mauve and the lip is white or pink with red spots but, as shown here, a white version can also be found.

Monkey Orchid, *Orchis simia*, is similar but it has smoother leaves and fewer flowers opening from the top downwards.

Naked Man Orchid, Rhodes April 6

Long-lipped Serapias, Greece April 2

Tongue Orchid

Serapias lingua, grows in olive groves, light woodland, dry and wet grasslands and maquis. It is common and widely distributed throughout the Mediterranean region as far west as Greece. 10–30 cm high, it flowers March to June. It is characterised by its elongated, tongue-like, central lobe and the swollen, grooved hump at the base of the lip. *Serapia neglecta* grows mainly in more acid soils in damp meadows, woodland and maquis. An uncommon species, it is found locally in southern France westwards to the Ionian Isles. 10–30 cm high, it flowers March to April. It is characterised by its elongated, oval central lobe and two parallel humps in the throat.

Long-lipped Serapias, *Serapias vomeracea*, grows in damp areas in woods, grasslands, hill-slopes, marshes and scrub. It is common and widely distributed throughout the Mediterranean region. 20–55 cm high, it flowers March to June. Characterised by its long, hairy lip, much longer than the helmet, and the bracts which are longer than the flowers.

Tongue Orchid, Greece, April 10

Serapia neglecta, France April 18

Common Rue, France May 23

Joint Pine

Ephedra fragilis, a shrub, grows on rocks, walls, hedges and bushy places. It is found in many parts of the Mediterranean region. Up to 5 metres high, it flowers February to April. A scrambling, numerously branched plant with rounded, jointed stems, it climbs through vegetation although the fragile, ribbed-top branches are often drooping. The cones are in pairs and the fruit is a bright red berry. The drug ephedrine is devised from members of this family.

The **Common Rue**, *Ruta graveolens*, a pot herb, grows on rocks, old walls and dry, limestone hills. It is often found cultivated and sometimes naturalised in the European Mediterranean region eastwards to Turkey. Up to 70 cm high, it flowers May to July. The leaflets are either oval and strongly aromatic or narrow and very faint smelling. The petals have smooth edges or are short-toothed and the fruits have rounded lobes. This plant is known to have antiseptic medicinal properties.

Joint Pine, France May 26

Fritillaria lusitanica, Ronda, Spain May 3

Fritillary

Fritillaria lusitanica grows in thickets, open woods, rocky or stony places and in alpine scree. It is found in Portugal and Spain. 10–30 cm high, it flowers March to July, according to altitude.

Variable in leaf length and flower colour and shape, it generally has bell-shaped flowers about 2 to 3 cm long and is browny-red or red-orange or purplish on the outside, and yellowy inside with narrow brown nectaries. The long, narrow, pointed leaves are ½ to 1 cm wide and have a greyish bloom on them. The flowers have a spermatic smell, and are pollinated by queen wasps.

Other rather similar species are found in the eastern Mediterranean; *Fritillaria messanensis*, 15–50 cm high with narrow leaves, a whorl of three near the flower and large oval nectaries, is found in scrub in Sicily, north Africa, Greece and Crete. A dwarfer species with broader leaves, *Fritillaria graeca* is commonest in the mountains in the Peloponnese and in Attica.

Fritillaria lusitanica photographed April 29

Snake's Head Iris, Brindisi, Italy April 3

Snake's Head Iris or Widow Iris

Hermodactylus tuberosus is a perennial growing in scrub, grassy banks and slopes and rocky, stony hills. It is quite common and found throughout the European Mediterranean region. It is also naturalised in southern England. 15–35 cm high, it flowers March to April.

This interesting iris has four, thin, soft, ribbed leaves which are longer than the flowering stem and which appear in autumn. It has a broad, leafy sheath and a single, bright greenish-yellow flower with dark purply-black, reflexed petals. The flowers are 4 to 5 cm long and fragrant. This plant grows from several, spreading, flesh, underground tubers and in well-drained, sunny places it will sometimes increase greatly.

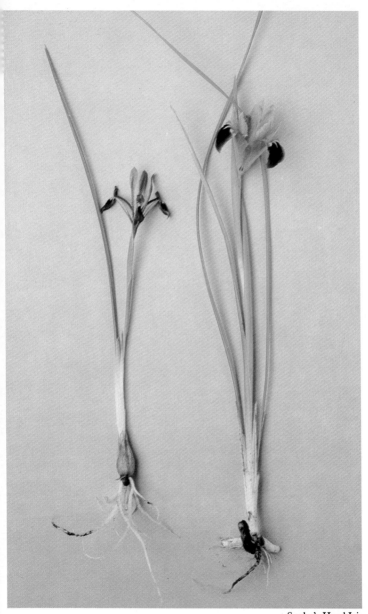

Snake's Head Iris

Wild Tulip, Aix, France April 15

Wild Tulips

Tulipa orphanidea grows on stony ground and in cultivated fields. It is found in the eastern Mediterranean region. 8–27 cm high it flowers March to April. This variable plant has up to 7 smooth, narrowish leaves and bright orange or orange-red flowers with a darker, basal blotch inside each segment.

Wild Tulip, *Tulipa sylvestris*, is a perennial which grows in vineyards, meadows, open woods and dry or grassy places. It, and its numerous subspecies, are found widely distributed throughout the Mediterranean region to Greece and northwards to Holland and England. 30–60 cm high, it flowers April to May. This very variable species usually has 4 long, narrow, grass-like leaves and yellow flowers with pointed petals, tinged green or reddish on the outside. The fragrant flowers have no basal spot and grow singly on a leafless stalk.

Wild Tulip (left), *Tulipa orphanidea* (right)

Allium nigrum, Algeciras, Spain May 14

Large Garlics

Nectaroscordum siculum is a tall, slender onion-like plant with stems up to 150 cm, sheathed at the base by a tubular leaf, and with floppy triangular leaves appearing from the bulb. The leaves appear in winter, the stems in early summer when they are crowned by an umbel of drooping bell-shaped flowers. Two subspecies are recognised, ssp. *siculum* with greenish-red flowers in the western Mediterranean, and ssp. *bulgaricum* with greenish flowers, tinged pale pink with a red spot inside, in the east, from Turkey to the Crimea, growing in damp, shady woods.

Allium nigrum grows in cultivated or waste ground, fields and among limestone rocks. It is widely distributed in the European Mediterranean region. 60–90 cm high, it flowers April to June.

It is a sturdy plant with 3–6 long, broadish leaves and a dense, round cluster of pale mauve or white flowers (up to 10 cm across) with green mid-veins. The anthers are yellowish.

Nectaroscordum siculum May 19

Rose Garlic, Narbonne, France May 26

Rose Garlic

Allium roseum grows in vineyards, dry open woods, grassy places, stony hills and gravelly places by the sea. It is common and found distributed in the Mediterranean region except Bulgaria. 15–40 cm high, it flowers April to June.

The largish, bell-shaped flowers are pale rose or violet (rarely white) and smell strongly of garlic. The bulb is surrounded by many small bulbils and some forms have bulbils in the flower cluster too.

Naples Garlic, *Allium neapolitanum*, grows in olive orchards, fields and grassy places. It is widely distributed throughout the Mediterranean region. 30–60 cm high, it flowers March to May. This tall, attractive plant has 2 to 3 broad, flat, hairless leaves projecting from the base and a cluster of long-stalked, shining white, cup-shaped flowers on a triangular sectioned stem. The petals have blunt, rounded tips and are longer than the stamens.

Naples Garlic May 1

Scilla peruviana, Spain May 12

Squills

Scilla peruviana grows in damp, grassy places and is found in the western Mediterranean region to Italy and Sicily. 20–50 cm high, it flowers April to June. This plant has numerous, strap-like leaves (sometimes with minute hairs on the margin) which project from the very large bulb. Long-stalked flowers create a dense, hemispherical cluster at the 50–100 cm stem head. Variable in size and flower colour, they range from dark purple or violet blue to white or pale brown (generally in North Africa).

Alpine Squill, *Scilla bifolia*, a perennial, grows in fields, scrub, meadows, grasslands and among rocks, ascending into mountains and often by melting snow. It is found widely distributed from Spain to Israel. 5–20 cm high, it flowers March to July. Characterised by its spear-shaped, blunt-tipped, shining, channelled leaves, usually a pair (occasionally 3 or 5), sheathing the stem. The violet to bright blue flowers are quite large and star-like and grow in a loose cluster.

Alpine Squill

Tassel Hyacinth, Sparta, Greece April 10

Tassel Hyacinth

Muscari comosum grows in dry meadows, olive orchards, cultivated fields and rocky ground. It is common and widely distributed in the Mediterranean region. 15–60 cm high, it flowers April to June.

This large grape hyacinth is a very variable plant characterised by its striking 'tassel' or tuft of bright, violet-blue sterile flowers at the top of the elongated spike and the widely-spaced, browny-green fertile flowers below. The long stalks of the sterile flowers are violet and curved upwards while the stalks of the fertile flowers spread horizontally. The bee-flies which are its usual pollinators, are initially attracted by the blue sterile flowers, find they lack nectar, and move down to the greenish flowers to feed. It has 3 to 6 long narrowish leaves. It is often eaten and can be seen for sale in markets.

In *Muscari pharmacusanum* a very similar, local Greek species, the sterile flowers are bright blue and stalkless or with very short stalks.

42

Tassel Hyacinth

Aphyllanthes monspeliensis, Nice, France April 20

Aphyllanthes

Aphyllanthes monspeliensis, a perennial, is found in dry, barren and rocky places in the western Mediterranean region to Italy. 10–25 cm high, it flowers April to July.

This strange-looking plant has small, scaly leaves reduced to a sheath enveloping the thin, ribbed, grey-blue, wiry stems which grow in a rush-like tuft from the base. Each stem has a head of starry blue flowers growing from greeny-brown bracts and each flower has six spreading, round-ended petals with a single dark blue vein running down the centre. The papery bracts contain the three-valved fruit.

Note that our specimen is rather more mauve than is generally found; usually the flowers are bluer than this.

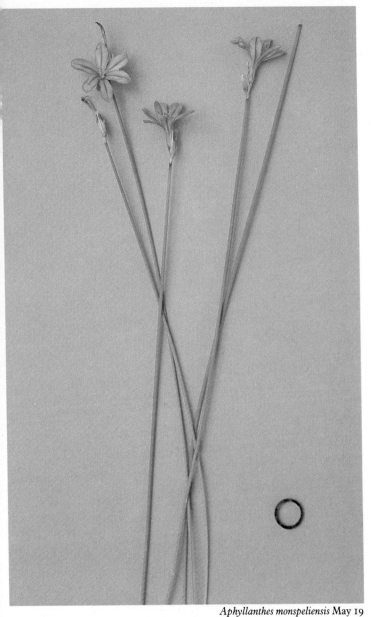

Aphyllanthes monspeliensis May 19

Barbary Nut, Spain May 10

Barbary Nut

Gynandriris sisyrinchium grows in dry places and hills up to 2000 metres. It is widely distributed throughout most of the Mediterranean region and eastwards to Pakistan although it is not found in France. 10–60 cm high, it flowers February to April.

This small iris is very variable in size with narrow, rush-like, grooved leaves sheathing the base and overtopping the flowers. The slender, wavy stem rises from a brown, scaly corm which is rather similar to *Iris reticulata*. The flowers grow in groups of 2–4 and vary in size from 1–3 cm. The spreading, outer petals are bright blue with a white or pale yellow patch towards the base; the inner petals are spear-shaped and upright. It is a very short-lived plant, with the flowers usually only opening in the afternoon, becoming faded by morning.

46

Barbary Nut, Kalamata, Greece April 18

Iris unguicularis, Greece April 4

Iris

Iris unguicularis grows in olive orchards, bushy places and stony ground. It is found in Greece and Crete, Rhodes, Turkey, Algeria and Tunisia. It grows from 10 to 25 cm high, and flowers December to April.

The winter-flowering Algerian form, better known to gardeners as *Iris stylosa* has long, slender, grass-like leaves about 1 cm wide and solitary, sweet-smelling, short-stalked flowers. The somewhat spreading outer petals are pale violet (sometimes whitish and violet at the tips) with mauve veins and a yellow patch with white edges at the base; the inner petals are mauve and more erect.

Iris cretensis sometimes regarded as a subspecies is very similar but less robust. Also, it has narrower leaves, 1–2 cm wide, and the smaller, pale flowers are stalkless. It is found in Crete, Rhodes and on the coasts of Turkey and Syria. Plants from Greece, where it is common in the Peloponnese, are intermediate in flower size and leaf width, and have striking bright bluish flowers with a bright yellow patch on the falls.

48

Iris unguicularis

Anemone pavonina, Greece April 16

Poppy or Crown Anemone

Anemone coronaria grows in olive groves, vineyards, fields and stony places. It is common and widely distributed throughout the Mediterranean region. 20–40 cm high, it flowers January to April. This striking anemone is easily distinguished by its large, solitary flowers each with 5–8 oval-shaped petals. The colour can vary from pink, red or, rarely, white to blue, lavender or purple, often with a contrasting colour in the centre. The red and purple forms are most common. The leaves differ from similar species by being deeply and numerously divided into narrow segments.

Anemone pavonina grows in olive groves, stony ground, fields and hillsides. It is sometimes common and is widely distributed in the Mediterranean region from France to Turkey, excluding Albania. 10–20 cm high, it flowers February to April. It has 7–9 broad, ovate, spear-shaped petals, often with a white base. The colour varies enormously from pink to purple or red and even, rarely, white.

Crown Anemone

Anemone hortensis, Nice, France April 21

Anemone

Anemone blanda grows among rocks, scrub and in bushy places up to 2000 metres and is found in the eastern Mediterranean region from Albania to Lebanon. 7–10 cm high, it flowers March to April.

Similar to the Blue Wood Anemone, *Anemone apennina*, the flowers are generally dark blue or white in Greece and uniformly pale blue in Turkey. The flowers are solitary with 9–15 narrow petals, which are hairless underneath. The stem leaves are dissected, also hairless underneath, and often tinged with violet. *Anemone hortensis* grows in hedges, fields, olive groves and grassy or stony places. It is quite widely distributed in the central Mediterranean region from France to Yugoslavia. 10–20 cm high, it flowers February to April. It is distinguished by its stem leaves which are bract-like, spear-shaped, usually undivided and some way below the flowers. The flowers have narrow, pointed petals usually spreading somewhat and varying in colour from purple to pink, red or white.

Anemone blanda March 27

Saponaria ocymoides, France May 20

Italian Catchfly

Silene italica, a perennial, grows in open, stony or sandy ground and is found distributed throughout the southern and central European region. 20–80 cm high, it flowers April to June.

The stems are minutely hairy on the lower section and the base leaves are spear-shaped. The ascending branches have flowers that are generally creamy white above and reddish or greenish below, with deeply divided petals.

Saponaria ocymoides, a perennial, grows in sandy or rocky places, in mountains. It is found in Spain and France. Up to 25 cm high, it flowers April to June.

This numerously-branched plant has hairy, ground-hugging or ascending stems with broad leaves at the bottom and narrower leaves at the top. The spreading flower cluster has conspicuous bright pink or pale purplish flowers and their stalks are hairy.

Italian Catchfly May 23

Oleaster, France May 20

Japanese Pittosporum and Oleaster

Pittosporum tobira, an evergreen shrub, grows in dry soil and cultivated ground. It is found planted throughout the Mediterranean region. Up to about 1 metre high, it flowers April to May. Often grown for ornament, this robust native of the Far East has smooth, leathery, oval or oblong leaves and flat-topped clusters of wonderfully fragrant, creamy-white or yellowish flowers with blunt petals.

Oleaster, *Elaeagnus angustifolia*, a spiny shrub or small tree, grows in dry soil or cultivated ground. It is found in southern Europe eastwards to Greece and northwards to central Russia. Up to 7 metres high, it flowers April to June. Often planted for ornament, this beautifully scented native of Asia has oblong leaves, green above and covered with silvery scales below. The twigs and dry yellow fruit are also covered with silvery scales.

Japanese Pittosporum, France May 12

Cyclamen repandum, Greece April 11

Cyclamen

Cyclamen repandum grows in woods, thickets, scrub, shady rocks and walls up to 500 metres. It is found widely distributed from southern France eastwards to Greece and Crete, also in Algeria. 10–15 cm high, it flowers March to May.

The leaves, which appear in early spring, are large, angularly heart-shaped and either deeply toothed or shallowly lobed. Usually bright green or dark green the leaves are either monochrome or blotched and marbled with white. The sweet-smelling flowers also vary in colour from bright rose to pink or, rarely, white with a darker blotch towards the throat; occasionally there is no 'eye'. It has a small, flattish tuber and roots from the centre.

Other closely related species are *Cyclamen balearicum* from southern France and the Balearic Islands which has small, whitish flowers with pink veins and *Cyclamen creticum* from Crete which has pure white (rarely pink) flowers and small leaves which appear in the autumn.

58

Cyclamen repandum April 22

Montpellier Milk-vetch, France May 26

Montpellier Milk-vetch

Astragalus monspessulanus grows in arid hills and rocky ground in the mountains. It is found in the Mediterranean region from Spain to Turkey. Up to 45 cm high, it flowers from May to June. The leaves can be as much as 20 cm long, comprising 10 to 15 leaflets, the flowering stems arising directly from the root. It is easily recognised by its dense clusters of rosy-purple flowers.

Annual Scorpion Vetch, *Coronilla scorpioides*, an annual, grows in fields, waste places and cultivated ground. It is common and found widely distributed throughout the Mediterranean region. 20–40 cm high, it flowers March to June.

A common weed, it is distinguished by long flower stalks with clusters of tiny, yellow flowers on the end, and its long, curved, narrow, jointed scorpion-like fruit pods. It has thickish, smooth, rounded, stalkless leaves composed of 3 leaflets, the central one four times the size of the side ones.

Montpellier Milk-vetch

Tangier Pea, Spain May 5

Wild Peas

Vicia tenuifolia grows in scrub and grassy waste places. It is widely distributed in the Mediterranean region. A perennial, up to 200 cm high, it flowers from April to June, or later in northern Europe where it is sometimes naturalised. The flowers are 12–18 mm long, the leaflets, in 5–13 pairs, linear or narrowly oblong.

Tangier Pea, *Lathyrus tingitanus*, an annual, grows in hedges, thickets, open woods, bushy places and screes. It is quite common and found in the western Mediterranean: Spain, Morocco and Algeria. A sprawling plant up to 100 cm high, it flowers April to July.

Often naturalised from cultivation this plant has large, scentless, rosy-purple flowers in clusters of 1–3 on long stalks. It is hairless and the pods shine when mature. It is very similar to the Everlasting Pea, *Lathyrus latifolius*, but has fewer, larger flowers in each cluster.

Vicia tenuifolia, Kos, Greece April 17

Bonjeania, Ardèche, France May 1

Bonjeania
Dorycnium hirsutum, a perennial sub-shrub, grows in bushy or grassy places at the edge of fields and rocks, stony slopes and sandy areas. It is common and found widely distributed in the European and Asiatic Mediterranean region. 20–50 cm high, it flowers April to July.

These shrubby plants have oblong, spear-shaped leaves that are covered in soft hairs, with 5 leaflets. The flowers grow in dense clusters of 5–10 and have very hairy calyxes which are half the length of the petals. The largish flowers are generally white, flushed with pink, and have a short, dark purple reel. This spreading, cottony plant has a woody base.

Bonjeania

Crimson Clover, France May 24

Crimson Clover

Trifolium incarnatum, an annual, grows in grassy or bushy places and cultivated ground. It is fairly common and widely distributed from France to Greece and also Great Britain and mainland Europe. 4–8 cm high, it flowers June to July.

This shortish, hairy plant has 3 obovate or rounded leaflets on each leaf stalk. The flower-heads grow in a cylindrical elongated cluster and vary in colour from bright scarlet to pink or creamy white with the sepal teeth spreading as they flower.

This clover is sometimes grown as a fodder crop and has become naturalised as a result of this.

Long-headed Clover, *Trifolium incarnatum* ssp. *molinerii*, is a pale-flowered subspecies commonly found on sea-side cliff tops, known in England on the Lizard Peninsula.

Crimson Clover

Star Clover, Spain May 12

Star Clover

Trifolium stellatum grows in dry places, stony slopes, roadsides and track and field edges. It is found throughout the Mediterranean region. 5–35 cm high, it flowers March to June.

Instantly recognisable, this hairy annual, densely covered with soft white hairs, has trefoil leaves with toothed leaflets and an oval-shaped flowerhead. The flowers are pale pink at first, then, as the flower fades the calyx grows and spreads outwards into a star shape, becoming a dark crimson colour, often with a white centre.

Star Clover May 25

Large Blue Alkanet May 11

Large Blue Alkanet

Anchusa azurea (synonym *Anchusa italica*), a perennial, grows in fields, tracksides, vineyards and waste places. It is widely distributed throughout the Mediterranean region. 20–150 cm high, it flowers April to August. This tall, herbaceous plant has a thick stem and long, spear-shaped leaves all covered in rough, bristly hairs. The bright blue or violet flowers grow in a loose, branched cluster. They have rounded, spreading petals and a brush-like tuft of white or pale blue hairs growing in the throat.

Purple Viper's Bugloss, *Echium lycopsis*, a biennial, grows in stony, sandy places, particularly on siliceous soils. It is found throughout the Mediterranean region. Up to 60 cm high, it flowers March to June. This attractive plant, has densely hairy stems and erect or spreading branches. The leaves are softly hairy and the large blue-violet flowers have a long, broad throat with two projecting stamens. Sometimes the flowers may be reddish, becoming bluish or white. The fruit is strangely warted.

Purple Viper's Bugloss May 26

Paeonia coriacea, Ronda, Spain

Peony

Paeonia coriacea, a perennial herb, grows in open woods and rocky places. It is found in the western Mediterranean region from Spain to Sardinia. 50 cm high, it flowers from April to May.

Very similar and also found in the western Mediterranean is *Paeonia broteroi* which differs in having rather glaucous leaves; flowers 8–10 cm across, red, with yellow stamen filaments. *Paeonia officinalis* has red flowers with red stamen filaments and leaves smooth above with 17–30 segments. It is found in southern Europe from Portugal to Romania. *Paeonia mascula*, commonest in Eastern Europe, but also known in France, has less divided leaves with 9–16 segments. *Paeonia rhodia* is a white-flowered peony, found in open pine forests in the hills on the island of Rhodes. It flowers in March and April. *Paeonia arietina* grows in bushy places or meadows and is found in the central and eastern Mediterranean region, though it is probably extinct in Greece. It is very similar to *Paeonia mascula* but has 15–17 wider, larger leaflets.

Paeonia arietina

Crown Daisy, Spain May 11

Crown Daisy
Chrysanthemum coronarium, an annual, grows in cultivated ground and waste places. It is found in the Mediterranean region and Portugal. 20–80 cm high, it flowers April to June. Frequently grown for ornament and sometimes naturalised, this plant has numerously branched stems. The oblong to obovate leaves are cut into linear segments and the flowers are yellow.

Corn Marigold, *Chrysanthemum segetum*, an annual, grows in cornfields and cultivated ground. It is found in many parts of the Mediterranean region as well as in Europe north to Scotland but is becoming rarer. 20–70 cm high, it flowers April to June. The smooth, blue-green, fleshy stems have few branches and although the lower leaves are deeply cut, the upper leaves are entire or toothed. The flowers are yellow.

Corn Marigold, France May 26

Pink Hawksbeard, Greece April 20

Pink Hawksbeard

Crepis rubra, an annual, grows in olive groves, herbaceous thickets and quarry rocks. It is found in the Mediterranean region from France to Turkey. 5–40 cm high, it flowers April to June. This plant has either a single or branched stem and narrow, slightly hairy, toothed or lobed leaves. The leafless, long-stalked flowerheads droop before flowering then produce large, pink or pink and white hawksbeard-like flowers.

Anacyclus valentinus, an annual, grows on disturbed ground. It is found in the western Mediterranean region. Up to 50 cm, it flowers April to June.

Anacyclus valentinus, Narbonne, France May 25

Golden Henbane April 17

Honeywort

Cerinthe major, an annual, grows in cultivated ground, field edges and stony places. It is common and widely distributed in the European Mediterranean region, Israel and North Africa. 15–50 cm high, it flowers March to June.

This sturdy plant has rounded, oblong, lower leaves that overlap and wrap around the stem and blunt, oval-shaped upper leaves with hairy margins. All the leaves are usually blotched with white swellings. The large, flask-shaped, yellow or cream flowers grow in drooping clusters and often have a browny-purple area at the base.

Golden Henbane, *Hyoscyamus aureus*, a perennial, grows in walls and cliffs and is found in Crete, Rhodes, Turkey and Egypt. 30–60 cm long, it flowers March to July. The irregularly lobed, toothed leaves are very hairy and sticky with egg-shaped blades. The bright yellow flowers with purple throats and protruding style and stamens grow in a loose cluster.

Honeywort, Spain May 15

Cytinus hypocistus, Greece April 22

Orobanche

Orobanche gracilis grows in fields and woods and is widely distributed in the Mediterranean region as far east as Turkey. 15–60 cm high, it flowers April to July. It is distinguished like other broomrapes by its lack of green colour in the leaves and stem: it is a parasite on members of the pea family. The leaves are like scales and the stem is reddish, hairy and glandular. The clover-scented flowers are yellowy-red outside and scarlet-flushed mauve inside.

Branched Broomrape, *Orobanche ramosa*, has a branched, flowering stem and pale blue flowers.

Cytinus hypocistus, is another strange, parasitic plant growing on the roots of the cistus species. 5–10 cm high, it flowers April to June. There are no green leaves but the stems are densely covered in bright orange or red overlapping scales. The flower heads, which push through the soil beneath the host plant, form a fleshy head of bright yellow flowers.

Orobanche gracilis, Sparta, Greece May 2

Mallow-leaved Bindweed, Cadiz April 20

Dwarf Convolvulus

Convolvulus tricolor, an annual, grows in hedges, fields, vineyards, road-sides and waste places. It is very common on the Costa del Sol and widely distributed in the western Mediterranean region to Greece. 10–30 cm long, it flowers March to May.

This spreading plant is recognised by its oblong leaves which taper at the base and its large, funnel-shaped flowers, on longish stalks, that are three-coloured: yellow at the throat, white in the middle and mauve-blue at the edge.

Mallow-leaved Bindweed, *Convolvulus althaeoides*, a perennial, grows in bushy, seaside areas, cultivated and waste ground and hills. It is widely distributed throughout the Mediterranean region. 80–180 cm high, it flowers April to June.

This climbing or trailing plant has hairy, triangular heart-shaped lower leaves and narrowly-lobed, finger-like upper leaves with longer hairs. The large, purply-pink flowers have darker centres.

Dwarf Convolvulus, France April 30

Campanula celsii, Greece May 16

Bell-flowers

Campanula celsii, a biennial, grows in rocks and cliffs and is found in south-eastern Greece and the Greek Islands. 20–30 cm high, it flowers April to July. This beautiful, climbing, branched bell-flower has variable leaves but the lower ones are generally up to 5 cm across, acutely egg-shaped, irregularly lobed and with a toothed, terminal lobe. The upper leaves are more roundedly egg-shaped, toothed and stalkless. The velvety, bell-shaped flowers are an intense lilac or lilac-blue colour and up to 3 cm across. *Campanula anchusiflora*, another spreading biennial, is similar but has a rosette of large, heart-shaped, shallowly lobed, toothed leaves at the base of the stem and small, tubular flowers of deep violet-blue.

Many other species are known from Greece, of similar general appearance to the above, but differing in technical characters, and often restricted to one small area.

Creeping Bellflower, *Campanula rapunculoides*, is another frequent and widely distributed species found in Spain and France.

Creeping Bellflower July 27

Birthwort, France June 20

Birthwort

Aristolochia clematitis, a perennial, grows in vineyards, stony or bushy places and waste ground, often near water. It is widely distributed in Europe, though probably native only in the south-east, and introduced elsewhere for medicinal use. 60–100 cm high, it flowers June to September. This hardy, striking plant has alternate, bluntly heart-shaped leaves and small clusters of flowers at the base of the upper leaves. The short-stalked, yellow flowers are swollen at the base and roughly tube-shaped with a flattened, projecting tip.

Round-leaved Birthwort, *Aristolochia rotunda*, grows in hedges, fields, bushy and stony places and cultivated land. It is quite common and widely distributed throughout the Mediterranean region excluding Morocco. 20–60 cm high, it flowers April to June. It is easily recognised by its stalkless, heart-shaped leaves, which encircle the stems. The small yellow, tubular flowers have a long, brown lip which bends over the opening.

Round-leaved Birthwort, Ardèche May 20

French Lavender, Cadiz May 15

French Lavender

Lavendula stoechas, a low shrub, grows in pine woods, open woods, sunny hillsides and dry stony places, particularly on siliceous soils. It is found throughout the Mediterranean region. 30–60 cm high, it flowers February to June.

This small, branched aromatic shrub has narrow, grey-green leaves covered on both sides with white, velvety hairs. It is easily distinguished by the topknot of long mauve (occasionally white) sterile bracts which project from the dense, oval cluster of much smaller, purple flowers immediately below it. The hairy bracts which bear the flowers are broad, papery and strongly purple-veined.

Renowned in ancient times for its healing properties, French lavender is still used in Islamic medicine in modern times. It is also used in France as a moth-deterrent and to perfume linen.

French Lavender, Perpignan May 27

Matthiola sinuata, Cadiz April 29

Sea Stocks

Matthiola sinuata, a biennial, grows near coasts and is found in southern and western Europe. 8–60 cm high, it flowers April to June.

Densely covered with fine white hairs this plant is woody at the base and has deeply lobed lower leaves. The uppermost leaves are entire and the flowers are pale purple.

Malcolmia littorea, a perennial, grows in sandy places and open pine woods near the sea and is found in the western Mediterranean region from Spain eastwards to Italy. 10–40 cm high, it flowers in April and May.

This woody plant has numerous flowering stems densely covered in white downy hair. The leaves are more or less stalkless and the flowers are purple.

Malcolmia littorea, Port Vendres, France May 28

Bellardia, Kos, Greece April 19

Bellardia

Bellardia trixago, an annual, grows in pine woods, fields, stony, grassy or sandy places, particularly if damp. It is widely distributed throughout the Mediterranean region. 10–80 cm high, it flowers April–June.

This stiff, erect, unbranched plant has oblong spear-shaped leaves with large, widely spaced teeth. The flower spike is densely covered in glandular, hairy bracts and the two-lipped flowers are clustered onto the four-sided spike. The large flower heads are whitish tinged with pink or yellow; the upper lip is hooded, the lower one is three-lobed and larger and there are two bosses in the throat.

Of similar habit, but with much smaller, darker flowers is *Parentucellia latifolia*, found in southern Europe northwards to north-west France.

Bellardia

Lavatera triloba, Cadiz May 19

Mallows

Lavatera triloba, a perennial, grows in ditches, stream-sides and damp sandy places, particularly in salt-rich soil. It is found in southern Spain and Portugal. 80–110 cm high, it flowers from April to June.

This shrubby, white or greyish plant has rounded or slightly three-lobed leaves giving a heart-shaped appearance. The musk-scented clusters of flowers are mauve-purple, sometimes flushed yellow with distinctive veins.

Lavatera trimestris, an annual, grows in cultivated land and sandy places by the sea. It is found in Portugal and eastwards to Greece. 90–120 cm high, it flowers in April and May. This tall plant has a rough, hairy stem and a large, baggy epicalyx. Large, bright pink flowers grow individually on the stems and have petals up to 5 cm.

Lavatera trimestris, Spain May 12

Biscutella megacarpaea May 16

Buckler Mustard

Biscutella laevigata, a perennial, grows on rocky, dry hills and grassy mountains, stony places and open woods. It is found in the Mediterranean region from Spain eastwards to Yugoslavia and also Morocco. 20–60 cm high, it flowers March to July.

This mustard-like, hairy plant has very variable leaves – sometimes shallowly toothed, sometimes deeply toothed, with or without hairs. The leaves at the base of the plant form a rosette, the stem leaves are small, sparse and stalkless. The yellow flowers have petals twice as long as the sepals. The most distinctive characteristic is the paired, flattened, disc-shaped valves of the ripe fruit, which resemble a pair of spectacles.

Biscutella megacarpaea, a perennial, grows on limestone rocks and is found in southern Spain. 80–100 cm high, it flowers in late April and early May.

Buckler Mustard, France

Yellow Lupin May 5

Lupins

Lupinus varius, an annual, grows in cultivated ground or rocky places, preferring sandy, acid soils. It is found in the Mediterranean region from Portugal eastwards to Greece and Crete. 20–70 cm high, it flowers in April and May. This silky or shaggy-haired plant is silvery or whitish with egg-shaped leaflets and irregularly whorled flowers: blue with a white and yellow, or purple, blotch.

Narrow-leaved Lupin, *Lupinus angustifolius*, is similar but has narrow leaflets and a spike of alternately arranged, small, dark-blue flowers.

Sweet Lupin or Yellow Lupin, *Lupinus luteus*, an annual, grows in cultivated ground and stony places. It is widely distributed in the Mediterranean region from Spain eastwards to Greece. 30–80 cm high, it flowers April and May. This hairy plant is similar to *Lupinus varius* with leaflets that are sparsely hairy above and flowers which are bright yellow. It is widely grown for cattle fodder.

Lupinus varius

Field Eryngo

Field Eryngo

Eryngium campestre, a perennial, grows in dry, stony places, waste ground, tracksides and plains. It is widely distributed in the Mediterranean region as far east as Turkey, and it is also a rare British native. 40–60 cm high, it flowers May to August. A spiny, thistly plant with diverging branches, it has long-stalked basal leaves, divided into spiny segments, and clasping stem leaves with spiny, heart-shaped bases. The flowers grow in a broad, dome-shaped cluster of narrow, pointed pale green bracts and purply or yellow-green flower heads.

Blue Eryngo, *Eryngium amethystinum*, grows on stony ground and mountains in the eastern Mediterranean region from Yugoslavia to Crete. 50–100 cm high, it flowers from July onwards.

Sea Holly, *Eryngium maritimum*, a perennial, grows on maritime sands and is found on the coasts of Europe northwards to 60°. 15–60 cm high, it flowers May to July.

Field Eryngo (left), Sea Holly (top)

Large Yellow Restharrow, Perpignan May 26

Large Yellow Restharrow

Ononis natrix, a small shrub, grows in dry stony places on the littoral. It is found widely distributed in southern and western Europe north-wards to northern France but is very rare in the Balkan peninsula. 20–60 cm high, it flowers April to June.

This attractive, numerously branched, dwarf shrub has densely hairy stems and variable leaflets – some oval, some linear. The large, yellow flowers, frequently veined with red or violet, grow in lax, leafy clusters.

Large Yellow Restharrow

White Asphodel, France May 20

White Asphodel

Asphodelus albus, a perennial, grows on dry hills, heaths and thickets and in mountainous meadows. It is found in the Mediterranean region from Portugal eastwards to Greece. 80–130 cm high, it flowers March to May. It is easily recognised by the narrow, stout, erect, unbranched stems and flat basal leaves which are V-shaped in section. The large white or pink, brown-veined flowers are borne in a dense, compact cluster at the top end of the stem.

Yellow Asphodel or King's Spear, *Asphodeline lutea*, grows in rocky, stony places in the central and eastern Mediterranean region. 80–100 cm high, it flowers April to May. This sturdy, unbranched plant has numerous, densely clustered, narrow leaves along the stem. Smooth-edged and stiff-pointed, they are triangular in section and sheath the base. The firm stem is topped by a long, dense, spike-like cluster of large yellow flowers.

Yellow Asphodel, Greece April 26

Drooping Star of Bethlehem, Turkey April 22

Drooping Star of Bethlehem

Ornithogalum nutans, a perennial, grows in fields, waste places, vineyards, grassy and cultivated ground. It is found throughout the European Mediterranean region and Asia Minor. 30–60 cm high, it flowers April to May. The green leaves are long, soft, narrow and grooved with a central white stripe. The large, greenish, bell-shaped flowers hang in a loose, one-sided, drooping cluster and are white inside with a green stripe at the back of each petal. The flower stalks are much shorter than the long, thin, pointed bracts.

Common Star of Bethlehem, *Ornithogalum umbellatum*, a perennial, grows in fields, groves, grassy or stony places and cultivated ground. It is found widely distributed throughout the Mediterranean region. 20–30 cm high, it flowers April to June. This short, spreading plant has narrow, limp, grooved leaves with a central white stripe. The star-like flowers with six petals are white with a green stripe on the back of each petal and form an umbel-like cluster on the leafless stem.

106

Common Star of Bethlehem May 11

Arum dioscoridis June 4

Dragon Arum
Dracunculus vulgaris grows in woods, scrub, rocky or bushy places and
waste ground. It is found in most parts of the Mediterranean region from
Portugal eastwards to Turkey and also Algeria. 80–100 cm high, it flowers
April to June. This strange-looking herbaceous plant has a stout stem,
mottled with purple patches, arising from a large, round tuber. The
purple-spotted palmate leaves have 9–15 oval leaflets, often mottled white.
The large spathe (up to 40 cm) is deep purple-brown inside and green
outside with a wavy, purple edge. The spadix is often just as long as the
spathe, deep reddish-purple, thick, fleshy and stinking.

    Arum dioscoridis grows in rocky, stony places and old walls. It is found in
the eastern Mediterranean from southern Turkey to Israel. 20–40 cm
high, it flowers in April and May. The large leaves have spear-shaped
blades; the spadix is dark purple, the spathe usually yellowish, spotted
with black, and the whole flower stinks of rotten meat.

Dragon Arum, Sicily April 28

Gladiolus communis, Castellorhizo, Greece April 10

Gladioli

Wild Gladioli are found commonly in the Mediterranean region; all have purplish-pink flowers of rather similar shape and size, and the species are not easy to distinguish from one another.

Gladiolus italicus is a native of France, Spain and north Africa, eastwards to Iran, growing commonly as a weed in cultivated ground such as cornfields. It is distinguished from other species by having anthers longer than the filaments. It grows up to 80 cm high, flowering March to July.

Gladiolus communis is similar, but has taller stems, is frequently branched and has 10–20 flowers in a spike. It grows in uncultivated fields and scrub and is found in southern Europe. Up to 100 cm high, it flowers from April to August.

Gladiolus illyricus grows on heaths, scrub and open woodland. It is found in southern and western Europe, northwards to southern England. 25–50 cm high, it flowers May to June. It is very similar to *Gladiolus communis* but much shorter and rarely branched.

Gladiolus illyricus, France May 30

Large Mediterranean Spurge, Corsica April 20

Large Mediterranean Spurge

Euphorbia characias, a perennial, grows in dry rocky places, field and track edges and on hills. It is found in the Mediterranean region from Spain eastwards to Crete and also Morocco and Libya. 30–80 cm high, it flowers March to May.

This tall, strong, hairy spurge is rather woody with long, leathery, spear-shaped leaves that are crowded together at the top end of the stem. The stems are thick and hairy, topped by cylindrical heads of flowers which are encircled by rounded, cup-like bracts, fused in pairs. The flowers are easily distinguished by their shallow, semi-circularly-shaped, reddish-brown glands with rounded tips. The fruit is densely woolly.

Tree Spurge, *Euphorbia dendroides*, another sturdy spurge, grows to 200 cm and has alternate leaves clustered all round the stem. The flower glands are similarly shaped but yellow and the fruit is smooth and hairless.

Euphorbia serrata, a perennial, is found in south-western Europe. 20–50 cm high, it flowers April to June.

Euphorbia serrata May 22

Hare's Tail, France May 26

Grasses

Vulpiella tenuis, an annual, grows in dry sandy places and is found in the western Mediterranean region. Up to 40 cm high, it flowers May to June. *Phleum subulatum*, an annual, grows in grassland and is found widely distributed in southern England and the Mediterranean from Spain to Turkey. 2–40 cm high, it flowers May to June. **Hare's Tail**, *Lagurus ovatus*, an annual, grows in dry places, particularly near the sea. It is found throughout the Mediterranean region. 5–50 cm high, it flowers April to June. This soft, delicate grass which has greyish-green leaves covered with woolly hairs and dense, white, silky flowering heads, is sometimes grown for ornament – the stems dried for winter decoration.

Aegilops ovata, an annual, grows in dry grass places and path-sides. It is found throughout the Mediterranean region. 10–30 cm high, it flowers April to June.

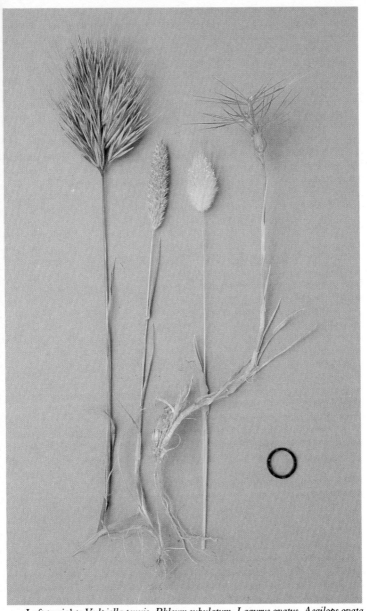

Left to right: *Vulpiella tenuis, Phleum subulatum, Lagurus ovatus, Aegilops ovata*

Giant Reed, France May 29

Giant Reed and other grasses

Arundo donax grows in damp places, ditches and watersides. It is found widely distributed in the Mediterranean region. 1½–5 metres high, it flowers May to June. This tall, bamboo-like perennial is frequently planted for windshields and used for thatching and basketry. *Bromus rubens* is found in south-west Europe and the Mediterranean region. 10–40 cm high, it flowers May to June. *Avena barbata* grows in dry waste places, roadsides and cultivated ground. It is found in the Mediterranean region from Spain eastwards to Turkey. 30–100 cm high, it flowers May to June. *Vulpia fasciculata* grows in open sandy places, particularly near the sea. It is found in south and western Europe and the Mediterranean region from Spain eastwards to Turkey. 8–50 cm high, it flowers May to June. Wall Barley, *Hordeum murinum* grows in dry, uncultivated waste areas and tracksides, and is found throughout the Mediterranean region. 5–50 cm high, it flowers April to June.

Left to right: *Bromus rubens, Avena barbata, Vulpia fasciculata, Hordeum murinum*

Long-beaked Storksbill

Tuberous Cranesbill

Geranium tuberosum grows in cornfields, vineyards, meadows and stony ground. It is found throughout the Mediterranean region. 20–40 cm high, it flowers March to June. This delicate cranesbill has a round, nut-like tuber from which narrow, long-stemmed, numerously divided and sub-divided leaves grow. Thin, minutely hairy and branched stems bear pinky-purple flowers with darker veins. The petals have a distinctive, rounded notch and are double the length of the hairy sepals.

Long-beaked Storksbill, *Erodium gruinum*, an annual, grows in fields, dry grasslands and sandy places by the sea. It is found in north Africa, Sicily and Greece eastwards to Israel. 30–50 cm high, it flowers February to May. This erect plant has thick, slightly hairy stems and two kinds of leaves: the lower ones are egg-shaped with a toothed margin; the upper ones are divided into three, triangularly-shaped, toothed leaflets with a longer central lobe itself often lobed. The petals of the violet flowers drop early and the fruits have a very long beak.

Tuberous Cranesbill April 30

Winged Sea Lavender April 30

Winged Sea Lavender

Limonium sinuatum, a perennial, grows in rocks and tracksides by the sea and sandy shores and is widely distributed throughout the Mediterranean region. 20–45 cm high, it flowers March to July. This attractive, robust plant has upright, winged stems and easily distinguishable rosettes of spear-shaped leaves with deeply rounded lobes. The blue-mauve calyx is much more noticeable than the whitish yellow petals. Winged Sea Lavender is widely cultivated for flower heads which, when cut and dried, will retain their colour for at least a year.

Other widely distributed species include: *Limonium ferulaceum*, which has no leaves at flowering time; *Limonium latifolium*, which has pale violet flowers in a long, dense cluster, and Matted Sea Lavender, *Limonium bellidifolium*, which is much smaller than the others.

Santolina chamaecyparissus grows in sandy, stony places and is found in the western and central Mediterranean region. 10–50 cm high, it flowers May to June.

Santolina chamaecyparissus, France June 1

Woolly Convolvulus, Lencate, France June 2

Woolly Convolvulus

Convolvulus lanuginosus, a perennial, grows on dry, calcareous rocks in lowlands and mountains. It is found in the south-western Mediterranean region. 5–30 cm high, it flowers April to June.

A silvery grey or whitish plant covered with woolly hairs, it has erect stems which are normally branched and often woody below. The leaves are linear and the numerous pink-striped flowers are crowded into dense clusters at the ends of the stems. The flowers are up to 2½ cm across and the calyx is covered with dense, spreading silvery hairs.

Woolly Convolvulus

Asteriscus maritimus, Spain May 8

Asteriscus

Asteriscus maritimus (synonym *Odontospermum maritimum*) grows in rocky places near the sea and dry places inland. It is found in the European Mediterranean and north Africa. Up to 20 cm, it flowers April to June. This soft, small shrub has numerous, many-branched, hairy stems. The hairy leaves are stalked and obovate and the large, deep yellow, solitary marigold-like flowers are borne on erect stems. The ray-florets are numerous, spreading and toothed at the top. *Pallensis spinosa* grows on dry, uncultivated ground and tracksides. It is found widely distributed in the Mediterranean region. Up to 60 cm, it flowers May to June. This softly hairy plant has hard, branched stems, spear-shaped leaves and yellow flowers.

Pallensis spinosa, France June 3

Phlomis purpurea, Cadiz May 21

Jerusalem Sage

Phlomis fruticosa, a shrub, grows in rocky and bushy places and is found in the Mediterranean region from France eastwards to Israel. 80–100 cm high, it flowers April to June. *Phlomis lychnitis*, a small shrub, grows on dry hills, rocks and stony places. It is found in south-western Europe. Up to 65 cm high, it flowers May to June. This plant has narrow, white-felted leaves and 4–8 whorls of yellow flowers with broad, oval bracts and shaggy-haired calyxes. *Phlomis purpurea*, a dwarf shrub, grows in hills and rocky places and is found in Spain. 80–120 cm high, it flowers from March to May.

This plant has leaves which are deeply wrinkled on the upper side and velvety white on the underside. The leafy flower spike has 2–5 whorls each comprising a maximum of eight pinky-purple flowers with soft, hairy, spineless bracts.

Phlomis herba-venti is similar but taller, with more purple flowers to each whorl and with stiff, curved, spiny bracts.

126

Phlomis lychnitis, France May 29

Genista scorpius, Spain

Brooms

Genista scorpius, a shrub, grows in lowlands, mountains and sunny, bushy hillsides and is found in France and Spain. About 100 cm high, it flowers in May and June. This erect, multi-branched plant has stout, spreading spines and small leaves. The little, orange-yellow flowers are mostly growing from the spines and the largish, hairless fruit is constricted between the seeds.

  Spanish Broom, *Spartium junceum*, grows in hedges and rocky, bushy places and is widely distributed in the Mediterranean region. 100–300 cm high, it flowers in summer. This plant is unmistakable because of its tall, smooth, rush-like, leafless stems. The narrow leaves at the base of the stems soon fall away. The large, attractive, sweet-smelling flowers are a strong yellow colour and grow in loose clusters at the end of the stems. The flattened fruit is silky haired at first, becoming hairless.

Spanish Broom, France June 1

Poplar-leaved Cistus, Spain May 22

Gum Cistus

Cistus ladaniferus, a shrub, grows in pine woods, copses and dry hillsides. Often common it is found widely distributed in the western Mediterranean region. 80–250 cm high, it flowers May to June. This tall, spindly plant has very sticky, fragrant branches with stalkless, spear-shaped leaves that are hairless on the upper side and white with woolly hairs on the underside. The large white flowers are borne individually at the end of short branches but sometimes appear as a cluster. They usually have a purple blotch at the base of each petal.

Poplar-leaved Cistus, *Cistus populifolius*, a shrub, grows in thickets, scrub, rocky and dry places and is found in Spain, France and Morocco. 130–200 cm high, it flowers May to June. A fairly tall, woody, aromatic plant, it has sticky branches and broad, oval-heart-shaped, pointed leaves, green but paler underneath. The large white flowers have a yellow centre and grow in small clusters with the scarlet buds drooping.

Gum Cistus, Spain May 16

Cistus Crispus, Spain May 19

Grey-leaved Cistus

Cistus albidus, a shrub, grows in scrub and rocky places, particularly on limestone soil. It is found in the western Mediterranean region. 40–100 cm high, it flowers from April to June. A very pretty, dense bush, faintly aromatic, it has stalkless, paired, narrow, oval leaves which are white-grey velvet on both sides with three protruding veins on the underside. The largish, crumpled flowers, rose or magenta-coloured, grow in clusters of 1–4 at the end of the branches.

Cistus crispus, a shrub, grows in woods, scrub and rocky places, particularly on acid soils and is found in the western Mediterranean region to Italy and Sicily. 30–50 cm high, it flowers April to June. This low-growing, highly aromatic, rounded bush has long-haired stems and grey-green, wrinkled leaves with wavy edges that are hairy, stalkless, veined and paired at their base. The purplish-crimson-pink flowers are bunched at the end of the branches and have a crumpled appearance.

Grey-leaved Cistus, Algeciras, Spain May 18

Echinops ritro, France June 1

Spanish Oyster Plant

Scolymus hispanicus grows in sandy places, waysides, waste land and cultivated land. It is found widely distributed in the Mediterranean region. 20–80 cm high, it flowers May to July. This biennial or perennial plant has narrowly winged stems and hairless, involucrul bracts with a narrow, papery margin.

Echinops ritro grows in dry often rocky places, and is found in most parts of the European Mediterranean. 20–60 cm, it flowers May to June. This cottony globe thistle generally has a branched stem and leaves with narrow spiny lobes. The flower heads are a rich blue and up to 4½ cm across.

Spanish Oyster Plant, France June 1

Dyer's Alkanet, France May 28

Dyer's Alkanet

Alkanna tinctoria grows in sandy and rocky places. It is found throughout the Mediterranean region. 5–30 cm high, it flowers April to June.

This greyish, shrubby perennial with ascendencing or procumbent stems has basal leaves that are linear, spear-shaped and upper leaves that are clasping. The small, bright blue flowers are about ½ cm across in leafy, forked spikes. The corolla is hairless and scale-less in the throat but has transverse swellings.

The thick root turns red when cut, and a pink dye can be made from it.

Dyer's Alkanet, France May 28

Sea Medick, France June 2

Sea Medick

Medicago marina, a perennial, grows in maritime sands on the shores of the Mediterranean, from Spain to Greece. 20–50 cm, it flowers May to June.

This easily recognisable littoral plant is usually growing prostrate over the sand. Densely leafy, the stems and foliage are covered with silvery or whitish woolly hairs. The pale yellow flowers grow in short-stalked clusters and the woolly-haired fruit forms a spiral with a small hole in the middle.

Sea Medick, France June 2

Prickly Pear, fruit, Corsica September 1

Prickly Pear or Barbary Fig

Opuntia ficus-indica grows in dry, arid and rocky places. It is common and found widely distributed throughout the Mediterranean region. 2–5 metres high, it flowers April to July.

This unmistakable cactus often forms an impenetrable bush with its spiny, swollen stems of flattened, racquet-shaped joints. The large, bright yellow flowers stem from the margins of the upper stem joints and the numerous sepals and petals are fused into a tube. The egg-shaped and egg-sized fruit is dull red, yellow or purple.

Prickly pear, a native South American plant, was reputedly introduced into Europe by Christopher Columbus. It propagates very easily and has become very common in the Mediterranean area. The dense hedges it forms are useful for keeping out animals and its delicious, edible fruits are commonly sold in the markets.

Prickly Pear, flower, Tenerife April 12

Oleander (red form), France June 7

Oleander

Nerium oleander, a shrub, grows in gravelly places, damp ravines and water edges. It is widely distributed around the Mediterranean region. 3–4 metres high, it flowers April to September.

This tall, strong plant has stiff, upright branches with long, narrow, leathery, pointed leaves in whorls of 3 or 4, grey-green in colour with numerous pairs of lateral veins. The largish flowers grow in clusters at the end of the stems, are bright pink (or sometimes white or red) and have spreading petals and a frilly throat. The long, ribbed fruits open into valves and the seeds have a fluffy tuft of hair.

Often grown as an ornamental shrub or hedge plant (as it forms dense thickets), its leaves contain a poisonous, milky juice. Thus in India, it is known as 'the horse killer' and is used as a funeral plant in both Hindu and Christian religions.

Oleander (pale pink form)

Century Plant, flower shoot just coming June 4

Century Plant

Agave americana grows on rocks, waste ground and roadsides and in planted hedges. It is widely distributed throughout the Mediterranean region. 8–10 metres high, it flowers June to August.

It is easily recognised by its huge rosettes (up to 4 metres across) of tough, very sharp, spiny-edged leaves. Stiff, blue-green in colour and triangular in section, they grow to 2 metres. The flowering stem is produced after about 10–15 years and rapidly grows about 10 metres in a month. The hundreds of green flowers are borne in the branched flower spikes and are only produced once in the plant's lifetime. After the flowering the plant dies but side shoots may live on.

A native of Mexico, the century plant has been naturalised in the Mediterranean region for over 200 years. A potent drink, pulque, can be made from the fermented juice which exudes from the young flower spike when cut.

Century Plant August 12

Pancratium maritimum, Corsica September 6

Sea Daffodil

Pancratium maritimum is common on sand dunes around the Mediterranean in Portugal and in south-western France. The large bulbs are deeply buried in the sand. The flowers, which are scented at night, appear from June to September. The seeds are black, large and covered with a spongy coating so that they float in the sea.

Polygonum maritimum, a perennial, grows on maritime sand and shingle on the shores of the Black Sea, the Atlantic (as far north as the Channel Isles) and the Mediterranean, from Spain to Turkey. 10–50 cm high, it flowers May to June.

This stout, woody plant has procumbent, branched stems and narrowly elliptical dark yellowish leaves, reddish brown at the base, with 8–12 conspicuous branched veins. The pink or white flowers grow singly or in axillary clusters of 2–4. The bracts are leaf-like and the nuts glossy.

Polygonum maritimum June 3

Aromatic Inula, Corsica September 7

Aromatic Inula

Dittrichia viscosa, a perennial, grows in olive groves, pinewoods, roadsides and rocky areas. It is widely distributed through the Mediterranean region. 40–130 cm high, it flowers from August to October.

This shrubby plant with its very strong, resinous smell has spear-shaped, sticky, hairy leaves, sometimes smooth, sometimes toothed. Erect leafy stems are clustered with bright yellow flowers at the top end.

Helichrysum stoechas, a perennial, grows in stony, rocky or sandy places. It is found in the Mediterranean region, eastwards to Turkey and also Morocco and Algeria. 10–50 cm high, it flowers April to June.

This woody-based plant has a spicy aromatic smell, like curry when crushed. The greeny and woolly-white leaves have inrolled margins and the woolly-white, unbranched stems bear dense, round clusters of small yellow 'everlasting' flowers.

Helichrysum siculum is very similar but is a smaller more spreading shrub with larger, everlasting flowers.

Helichrysum stoechas, France June 6

Cotton Weed, Corsica September 12

Cotton Weed

Otanthus maritimus, a perennial, grows in sand dunes, coastal shores and shingle. It is found throughout the Mediterranean region. 10–45 cm high, it flowers May to August.

A stout-stemmed, spreading plant, covered in thick, silvery-white down, it has numerous, fleshy, oblong-toothed leaves, densely bunched together. The small clusters of yellow flowers are grouped at the ends of the branches and are covered in thick hairs.

Purple Spurge, *Euphorbia peplis*, an annual, grows on sandy shores and is found in the Mediterranean region from France eastwards to Greece. 3–5 cm high it flowers July to September.

This low, fleshy, hairless plant has crimson stems and grey or purplish, opposite oblong leaves. The stalked flowers grow along the stems.

Purple Spurge, France July 2

Autumn Squill, Corsica September 14

Autumn-flowering Narcissus
Narcissus serotinus grows in dry hills, scrub and rocky places and is found throughout the Mediterranean region, excluding France. 15–25 cm high, it flowers September to October.

This lovely sweet-smelling, late-flowering narcissus has very thin slender leaves which appear in spring and have disappeared by the time the plant flowers. The slender stems carry a solitary flower (occasionally two), which has white petals and a narrow, bright yellow crown.

Autumn Squill, *Scilla autumnalis*, a perennial, grows in rocks, hills and dry grassy places near the sea. It is found throughout the Mediterranean region. 10–25 cm high, it flowers August to October.

This low, autumn-flowering squill has thin, very narrow, shining leaves stemming from the roots and appearing after the flowers. The roughly-hairy stem is leafless and the purplish-blue, star-like, bractless flowers group in clusters but then spread.

Autumn-flowering Narcissus

Naked Boys or Colchicum

Colchicum, Corsica September 16

Colchicum bivonae grows on rocky hillsides and in grassy or stony places. It is found in the Mediterranean region from Italy eastwards to the Greek Islands and also Algeria and Tunisia. 10–15 cm high, it flowers August to October. The 5–9 broad, shining leaves emerge in spring. *C. variegatum* is commonest on the Greek Islands and in south-west Turkey. It has starry flowers and wavy-edged leaves.

Other autumn crocuses are Meadown Saffron, *Colchicum autumnale*, which has pale purple flowers that appear, without leaves, in August or September; *Colchicum neapolitanum*, which is similar to Meadow Saffron but smaller with pinker flowers and *Colchinicum steveni* which has 5–7 leaves and pink or white flowers.

Colchicum species were regarded as a dangerous but important medicinal plant in ancient times but now they are regarded as important in horticultural and agricultural genetics because of the effect their substance, colchicine, has on chromosomes.

Colchicum

Sowbread, Corsica September 16

Sowbread

Cyclamen neapolitanum grows in woods and rocky or bushy places, particularly on limestone. It is found in the Mediterranean region from France eastwards to Turkey. 10–20 cm high, it flowers July to November. The leaves of this faintly scented cyclamen are very varied: rounded or shallowly lobed, they are often purply underneath and marbled with silver on top. The large tubers only root from the upper surface. The flowers vary in colour from pale pink to white with a darker blotch at the base of each reflexed petal.

Cyclamen cilicium grows in pinewoods and rocky hillsides up to 2000 metres, and is found in southern Turkey. 10–15 cm high, it flowers September to November. This pretty cyclamen has a large, round tuber and rounded, heart-shaped leaves, darkish green mottled with pale yellowy-green on the top and pinky-brown on the underside, with dark pinky stems. The pale, leafless stems bear a solitary white flower with a dark pink blotch at the base of the reflexed petals.

Cyclamen cilicium September 8

INDEX

Acacia dealbata 4
Aegilops ovata 114
Agave americana 144
Alkanet, Large Blue 70
Alkanna tinctoria 136
Allium neapolitanum 38
Allium nigrum 36
Allium roseum 38
Alpine Squill 40
Anacyclus valentinus 76
Anchusa azurea 70
 italica 70
Anemone 52
Anemone apennina 52
 blanda 52
 coronaria 50
Anemone, Crown 50
Anemone hortensis 52
 pavonina 52
Annual Scorpion Vetch 60
Aaphyllanthes monspeliensis 44
Aristolochia clematitus 86
 rotunda 86
Aromatic Inula 148
Arum dioscoridis 108
Arundo donax 116
Asphodeline lutea 104
Asphodelus albus 104
Asphodel, White 104
 Yellow 104
Asteriscus maritimus 124
Astragalus monspessulanus 60
Autumn-flowering narcissus
 152
Autumn Squill 152
Avena barbata 116

Barbary Fig 140
 Nut 46
Barley, Wall 116
Barlia robertiana 16
Bellardia 92
Bellardia trixago 92
Bell-flowers 84
Biennial Alexanders 21
Birthwort 86
Birthwort, Round-leaved 86
Biscutella laevigata 96
 megacarpaea 96
Blue Eryngo 100
Bonjeania 60
Branched Broomrape 80
Bromus rubens 116
Broom, Spanish 128
Buckler Mustard 96

Campanula anchusiflora 84
 celsii 84
 rapunculoides 84
Catchfly, Italian 54
Century Plant 144
Cerinthe major 78
Chrysanthemum coronarium 74
 segetum 74

Cistus albidus 132
 crispus 132
Cistus, Grey-leaved 132
 Gum 130
Cistus ladaniferus 130
Cistus, Poplar-leaved 130
Cistus populifolius 130
Clover, Crimson 66
 Star 68
Colchicum 154
Colchicum autumnale 154
 bivonae 154
 neapolitanum 154
 steveni 154
 variegatum 154
Common Rue 28
Convolvulus althaeoides 82
 lanuginosus 122
 tricolor 82
Convolvulus, Woolly 122
Corn Marigold 74
Coronilla scorpioides 60
Cotton Weed 150
Cranesbill, Tuberous 118
Creeping Bellflower 84
Crepis rubra 76
Crimson Clover 66
Crown Daisy 74
Cyclamen 58
Cyclamen balearicum 58
 cilicium 156
 creticum 58
 neapolitanum 156
 repandum 58
Cytinus hypocistus 80

Daffodil, Sea 146
Dittrichia viscosa 148
Dorychium hirsutum 64
Dracunculus vulgaris 108
Dragon Arum 108
Dwarf Convolvulus 82
Dyers' Alkanet 136

Echinops ritro 134
Echium lycopsis 70
Elaeagnus angustifolia 56
Ephedra fragilis 28
Erodium gruinum 118
Eryngium amethystinum 100
 campestre 100
 maritimum 100
Eryngo, Blue 100
 Field 100
Euphorbia characias 112
 dendroides 112
 peplis 150
 serrata 112

Fennel, Giant 20
Ferula communis 20
Field Eryngo 100
French Lavender 88
Fritillaria graeca 30
 lusitanica 30
 messanensis 30

Fritillary 30

Gagea amblyopetala 6
 chrysantha 6
 peduncularis 6
Garlic, Naples 38
 Rose 38
Genista scorpius 128
Geranium tuberosum 118
Gladioli 110
Gladiolus communis 110
 illyricus 110
 italicus 110
Golden Henbane 78
Grey-leaved Cistus 132
Gum Cistus 130
Gynandriris sisyrinchium 46

Hare's Tail 114
Helichrysum siculum 148
 stoechas 148
Henbane, Golden 78
Hermodactylus tuberosus 32
Himantoglosssum
 longibracteatum 16
Holly, Sea 100
Honeywort 78
Hordeum murinum 116
Hyacinth, Tassel 42
Hyascyamus aureus 78

Iris cretensis 48
 reticulata 46
Iris, Snake's Head 32
Iris stylosa 48
 unguicularis 48
Iris, Widow 32
Italian Catchfly 54

Japanese Pittosporum 56
Jerusalem Sage 126
Joint Pine 28

King's Spear 104

Lagurus ovatus 114
Large Blue Alkanet 70
 Garlics 36
 Mediterranean Spurge 112
 Yellow Restharrow 102
Lathyrus latifolius 62
 tingitanus 62
Lavatera triloba 94
 trimestris 94
Lavender, French 88
 Matted Sea 120
Lavendula stoechas 88
Limonium bellidifolium 120
 ferulaceum 120
 latifolium 120
 sinuatum 120
Long-beaked Storksbill 118
Long-lipped Serapias 26
Lupin, Sweet 98
 Yellow 98

Lupinus angustifolius 98
  luteus 98
  varius 98

Malcolmia littorea 90
Mallow-leaved Bindweed 82
Mallows 94
Marigold, Corn 74
Matted Sea Lavender 120
Matthiola sinuata 90
Medicago marina 138
Mimosa 4
Mirror of Venus 12
Montpellier Milk-vetch 60
Muscari comosum 42
  pharmacusanum 42

Naked Boys 154
Narcissus serotinus 152
Nectaroscordium siculum 36
Nerium oleander 142

Odontospermum maritimum 124
Oleander 142
Oleaster 56
Ononis natrix 102
Ophrys bombyliflora 12
  ferrum-equinum 8
  fusca 14
  lutea 14
  scolopax 10
  specul..n 12
  sphegodes 8
  tenthredinifera 10
Opuntia ficus-indica 140
Orchid, Bumble Bee 12
  Early Spider 8
  Giant 16
  Horseshoe 8
  Loose-flowered 18
  Mirror 12
  Monkey 24
  Naked Man 24
  Pink Butterfly 22
  Sawfly 10
  Sombre Bee 14
  Tongue 26
  Woodcock 10
  Yellow Bee 14

Orchis italica 24
  laxiflora 18
  papilionacea 22
  simia 24
Ornithogalum nutans 106
  umbellatum 106
Orobanche 80
Orobanche gracilis 80
  ramosa 80
Otanthus maritimus 150

Paeonia arietina 72
  broteroi 72
  coriacea 72
  mascula 72
  officinalis 72
  rhodia 72
Pallensis spinosa 124
Pancratium maritimum 146
Parentucellia latifolia 92
Pea, Tangier 62
Peas, Wild 62
Peony 72
Phleum subulatum 114
Phlomis fruticosa 126
  herba-venti 126
  lychnitis 126
  purpurea 126
  Hawksbeard 76
Pittosporum tobira 56
Polygonum maritimum 146
Poplar-leaved Cistus 130
Poppy 50
Prickly Pear 140
Purple Spurge 150
  Viper's Bugloss 70

Reed, Giant 116
Restharrow, Large Yellow 102
Round-leaved Birthwort 86
Ruta graveolens 28

Sage, Jerusalem 126
Santolina chamaecyparissus 120
Saponaria ocymoides 54
Scilla autumnalis 152
  bifolia 40
  peruviana 40
Scolymus hispanicus 134

Sea Daffodil 146
  Holly 100
  Medick 138
  Stocks 90
Serapias lingua 26
Serapias, Long-lipped 26
Serapias neglecta 26
  vomeracea 26
Silene italica 54
Silver Wattle 4
Smyrnium perfoliatum 20
  rotundifolium 20
Sowbread 156
Spanish Broom 128
  Oyster Plant 134
Spartium junceum 128
Spurge, Large Mediterranean
  112
  Purple 150
Squills 40
Star Clover 68
Star of Bethlehem, Common
  106
  Drooping 106
  Yellow 6
Stocks, Sea 90
Storksbill, Long-beaked 118
Sweet Lupin 98

Tangier Pea 62
Tassel Hyacinth 42
Trifolium incarnatum 66
  stellatum 68
Tuberous Cranesbill 118
Tulipa orphanidea 34
  sylvestris 34
Tulip, Wild 34

Vicia tenuifolia 62
Vulpia fasciculata 116
Vulpiella tenuis 114

Wall Barley 116
White Asphodel 104
Winged Sea Lavender 120

Yellow Asphodel 104
  Lupin 98

Other titles in this series:

Birds

Butterflies

**Wild Flowers of Mountain
and Moorland**

Coastal Wild Flowers

Herbs and Medicinal Plants

Seashells and Seaweeds

**Wild Flowers of Roadsides
and Waste Places**

Weeds

Trees

Mushrooms

Woodland Wild Flowers

Roger Phillips has pioneered the photography of natural history which ensures reliable identification. By placing each specimen against a plain background he is able to show details that would otherwise have been lost if it had been photographed solely *in situ*. Such is the success of this technique that his books, which include *Mushrooms*, *Wild Food* and *Freshwater Fish*, have sold over a million copies worldwide. He is also the winner of numerous awards, including three for best produced and best designed books and the André Simon prize for 1983 for *Wild Food*.

Martyn Rix took a degree in botany at Trinity College, Dublin and then went on to Cambridge. After a further period of study in Zurich he became resident botanist at the Royal Horticultural Society's gardens at Wisley for several years. He is now a freelance writer.

Nicky Foy did an English degree at Queen Mary College, before training to be a teacher. After completing a one-year post-graduate degree she taught English for seven years and was Head of the Sixth Form at an inner London comprehensive. In 1982 she left teaching to become a freelance writer, researcher and editor.

Acknowledgements

We should particularly like to thank Jill Bryan for her help with the lay-out and production of the books.

ELM TREE BOOKS
Published by the Penguin Group
27 Wrights Lane, London W8 5TZ, England
Viking Penguin Inc., 40 West 23rd Street, New York, New York 10010, USA
Penguin Books Australia Ltd, Ringwood, Victoria, Australia
Penguin Books Canada Ltd, 2801 John Street, Markham, Ontario, Canada L3R 1B4
Penguin Books (NZ) Ltd, 182–190 Wairau Road, Auckland 10, New Zealand
Penguin Books Ltd, Registered Offices: Harmondsworth, Middlesex, England
First published in Great Britain 1988 by Elm Tree Books
Copyright © 1988 by Roger Phillips
All rights reserved.
ISBN 0-241-12435-2
ISBN 0-241-12436-0 Pbk
Printed and bound in Spain by Cayfosa Industria Gráfica, Barcelona